# You Don't Need to Conduct the Orchestra:

## Lessons on Letting Go, Trusting and Allowing

# You Don't Need to Conduct the Orchestra:

## Lessons on Letting Go, Trusting and Allowing

# Jack Armstrong

**Author of *Lessons from the Source***

**Wisdom from the Source Publications**

You Don't Need to Conduct the Orchestra:
Lessons on Letting Go, Trusting and Allowing

Jack Armstrong. (You Don't Need to Conduct the Orchestra: Lessons on Letting Go, Trusting and Allowing)

Wisdom from the Source Publications

Printed in the United States of America

*For all of us who are learning to let go.*

Greetings,

One of the biggest challenges for those of us on the spiritual path is integrating – and actually living! – the spiritual truths we understand and believe.

For me, and I'm guessing for you as well, one of the toughest parts of that is being able to let go of my own need to make things happen in a way that my human mind has decided would be best – and then to trust and allow the perfection of the Universe to unfold.

When we're *not* able to let go, and (surprise, surprise!) things don't work out the way we think they should, we begin to struggle, and that can generate negative emotions like doubt or concern or fear or frustration. And those, in turn, can cause us to struggle even more.

One of the most consistent messages in the teachings I've been transcribing over the years is a reminder that, as spiritual beings, we can let go of the struggle, that our human minds are not completely in control of what happens in our lives, and that we don't have to understand exactly what's going on or find new ways to accomplish what seems to us to be so darn important.

The reminders sometimes have been so frequent that I've felt like Source was hitting me over the head with a cosmic two-by-four, but the message is always gentle and presented in ways that help me stop and center myself in what I already know.

One particular sentence that came in a paragraph I wrote down in 2005 keeps popping up in my mind, and it seems to me to summarize all of the reminders: ***You don't need to conduct the orchestra.*** The implication, of course, is that the orchestration is already taken care of.

The passages I'm sharing with you here are some of my favorites, and I trust they will be meaningful to you, as well. Much love and many blessings.

Jack Armstrong

**Accept, rejoice in and surrender to the divine orchestration**, the perfection that your human mind cannot see or even begin to comprehend – and you do not need to. Simply trust it and surrender to it (while doing what you know to do in the physical world) and then release any concerns or uncertainties about what will happen when, or how it will happen, or who will be involved. Your human mind does not need to know or understand or orchestrate or comprehend. Its role is simply to trust and allow.

∞

**What an interesting dynamic there is in the human journey.** The goodness, the perfection, the blessings are always with each person. Always. Yet the challenge of the journey is to recognize the obstacles and obstructions that the human mind attempts to create to them.

Life on earth is a power game. The true power is placid and ever present. It is peaceful and loving and joyous. It is your true essence, and it will overcome any obstacle if you only will allow it.

But the obstacles are temporary creations of your human mind when it assigns power to situations that have none. They truly have none. Yet the human mind assumes that they do, and it responds to this perceived, but illusionary power by trying to fight it and prove its own superiority.

It is like fighting against a phantom. You have all the power – always. If you can simply accept and understand and enjoy and relish that truth, the phantoms disappear, for their illusionary nature is revealed and exposed, and they dissolve into nothingness.

It is your human mind's response to the illusions that it has created that is the key. Your mind exercises its own free will. It makes the decisions about how to respond, how to experience the illusions that can seem so real.

The battle is within the mind. Think of the power of nonviolence in the physical world. It is powerful and ultimately rules because it does not respond to the negativity in like manner. It is tranquil and peaceful and non-reactive. This is an expression/an example in the physical world of the choice available to your mind in every situation.

Accept your true power and allow it to hold sway in every situation. You can make the decision, always. Imagine the heavyweight champion of the world feeling a challenge to his reign from a pesky and petulant two year old who stomps his feet and insists he is right. If the champion (representative in this illustration of unquestioned power and rule) were to allow the child to hold sway, and he became worried and frightened by the child's assertion of power, and if he responded to the false power which he allowed to gain control of the situation in his own mind and tried to fight it on equal terms, the world would respond with mockery and disbelief.

This may be a silly example, but accept it and contemplate it. You have the uncontested power of your true being as my expression. Nothing can overcome it unless you allow it to.

∞

**You are so near, yet are feeling so far.** All you need do is let go of your feeling of the need to make things happen and turn it all over to me. Finally, simply, effortlessly let go.

Remember divine order and effortless perfection. They are real. They are the way the universe and all living things – and your life – work, but the key is letting go of that human need to be in control. For plants and animals there is no issue, for they do not have the challenges or blessings of a mind that constructs scenarios – either positive or negative – for their existence.

Acceptance and trust are not only easy – that is all they know. There is no struggle at all – even in the face of adversity or threats to the continuation of their lives on the planet.

The human mind is a blessing much more than a curse, for it can be the agent, the connection point, with me that allows effortless perfection to be a given in your life.

It is a curse only when you allow it to be. It will raise all manner of objections to your desires and will concoct imaginary reasons for why they cannot/will not become reality. You can cast your vote for or against its protestations, for it is always your choice.

Step back now and make the choice for the rest of your journey by simply letting go and allowing. Set your intentions through meditation and by seeking my guidance, and then celebrate effortless perfection and watch your blessings unfold before you in effortless perfection. I love you. Be at peace.

∞

**The major struggles of the human mind are its need to be in control and to make things happen on its own terms** – believing that it knows, and can accomplish on its own, what is in its best interests. When those beliefs become disproven, over and over again, negative emotions arise – out of frustration at not being able to make things happen, or fear that something external will derail its plans, or anger at someone or some condition it believes has prevented its interpretation of its highest good to happen.

The question of manifesting good relates to that basic dichotomy of your identities. On the one hand, the good you desire is always available and easily accessible to your true beingness; on the other, it often seems out of reach in spite of the efforts of the human mind to accomplish it on its own.

Guidance is your true being, at the highest levels, gently nudging your struggling human identity to help it understand and move in an appropriate direction. That guidance is always available and is the most important factor in helping your human identity to understand truth and let go of its futile attempts to be in control.

The Kingdom can be realized and lived during your physical journey when the struggle is released, the guidance of your true beingness is heard and accepted and followed, and you can live and express your true essence.

Difficulties in manifesting the good that is already there for you are due to the struggle – to the human mind's need to make things happen on its own. When the struggle is gone, and you can simply be certain that the good is yours, ask for the guidance that is always there, and then trust and allow the good to unfold – without any restrictions of how or when or who.

The human journey is about learning to let go of the struggle and allow life to unfold perfectly and effortlessly, even though the human mind cannot understand it. It does not need to!! Simply claim and accept your good and blessings, which are always yours as a spiritual being in the Kingdom, and then trust and allow, without any struggle.

∞

**You have struggled with the matter of manifesting your dreams**, yet it feels to you like your progress is slight, and you become concerned and frustrated.

The key words here are "struggled," "concerned" and "frustrated." Concern and frustration, of course, are negative emotions generated by your human consciousness, and you have allowed them to gain a toe-hold in your mind and emotions. They have been generated and have been given power because of what you have perceived as an inordinate delay in realizing the success that you know is possible and to which you are entitled. And you have struggled. Whether the struggle has caused the negative emotions or has resulted from them does not matter. They are closely related.

If you truly believe that, with me, all things are possible, there would be no need to struggle. If you are my expression, and if my will for you is the realization of the desires which I have planted in your human consciousness, and if, with me, all things are possible, then there is no need to struggle or fret or force the issue.

Yet you still feel, to some extent, that you are depending on people and conditions and circumstances in the physical world for your success, and those feel out of your control, so you begin to struggle and to express concern and frustration.

It is time to let go.

God makes a way where there is no way. It is the God within who does the acts. Accept these truths. Absorb them and establish them in your consciousness, and then let go of your struggles and concerns and frustrations.

You have not been able to find the way, working strictly on your own (that is, using only the devices of your human consciousness and relying on the positive reactions of others "out there"). It does not appear to you that there is a way, though you want to believe there is. I can and will and want to make the way for you, if you can let go of your need to make it on your own. If you will let go of the struggle and let me do the works (better said, let us do them together, or let me do them through you – my expression on the physical plane), the way will appear before you.

∞

**Allow it all to unfold, under my guidance, in the certainty of perfection.** Your human mind does not have to take on full responsibility for perfection. Yes indeed it does try – and try and try – but of course perfection simply is. Always. In all things.

What an essentially simple concept, yet the human mind sees it as so complex that its tendency is either to throw up its emotional hands in disbelief or to deny its possibility ("clearly, given what is happening in my life, there is no way that could possibly be true") and set to work trying to achieve perfection on its own.

How unfortunate. If the mind of man can simply (yes, simply) let go of its efforts and surrender to the perfection of all things, there would be no struggle or pain or grief or frustration or anger or fear or worry or desperation – or any other emotion based on the human mind's inability to attain perfection (through its own limited perception of the concept) by its own devices.

I've got things covered, to use the parlance of the time in the English language. If someone you knew and trusted implicitly were to say that to you in regard to some issue you were facing and over which that person had influence and authority, it would be easy and natural for you to let go of your concern, certain that things would be taken care of, and move on to whatever the next thing was on your list of issues to be concerned about.

Why, then, can you not accept that same assurance from me and move ahead, comfortably and confidently with whatever undertaking you might be involved in or concerned about?

The only power in the Universe. The one true power. The source of all good – and all creation. Do you find any limitation or deficiency in those definitions of me with which you are so familiar? Of course not, for there are none.

I do have every situation in your life – from the seemingly most complex to those you seldom if ever even think about – covered so perfectly that you can feel totally justified and confident and secure in letting go not only of any concern or attachment to them, but also of any need to figure out how you, as a human entity, can do a better job than I.

You are free of all that nonsense. Try for a moment to feel the comfort and lightness and joy of that freedom. They are yours – in every moment of "time" on the earth plane and throughout eternity.

I will be helping you. I am now and always have been. The guidance is always there – perfect, unquestionable guidance – and the way is always being made clear, if only you will get out of the way and allow perfection to unfold effortlessly. No effort on your part.

By effort, of course, I mean struggle of any kind. Yes, you will need to follow my guidance and take actions of various kinds, but you are allowing me to take them through you. It is the God within that doeth the works.

Freedom is a hard concept for you to accept, isn't it? It is much easier for the human mind to accept in general than is perfection, yet they work hand in hand, one with the other, and all you need do is to allow your limited human cognition to let go, surrender, accept and allow. Enjoy the freedom and perfection of your day. I love you.

∞

**You need not struggle.** It is not your responsibility to "figure it out." It is all about acceptance. It is about peace and joy and love. It is about feeling and expressing my presence and the essence of me in the world in each and every moment.

But, your conscious mind is protesting: "I can't do that in each and every moment, because there are distractions and things to do and unexpected interruptions."

You are allowing your human mind to dictate the terms. You are falling victim to its need to be in control. It fears relinquishing any of its authority over you, for if it let go of all control there would be no need for its presence or involvement.

That, of course, is pure folly, for you are on a journey in the physical world, and your human mind and body are absolutely essential companions. Without them, you would be in spiritual form exclusively.

Your human mind is very accepting of, and comfortable with, the fact that the physical body will die and end its journey, but it does not entirely accept its own finite role as your spiritual being's second companion on the journey.

It is very difficult for your human consciousness (which is separate from your human body, because your spiritual being is responsible for its perfect functioning, and your human mind is then free to find its own challenges and struggles) to accept its own limitations, for it always has a need and compulsion and strong desire to control all aspects of your life on earth.

Any limitations of your physical mind or body are illusions created by the human mind to justify its existence.

If there are perceived limitations, the human mind takes on the self-anointed "responsibility" to overcome them, and from this sense of responsibility (and impossibility) come the struggles of your life – the fears and doubts and uncertainties and inadequacies and lack that you have allowed your human consciousness to struggle with.

Because it feels a responsibility to overcome all of its self-created limitations, the struggle continues until the end.

Similarly, the human mind does not focus on the finite nature of the journey, because that would mean an end to its rule and its struggle.

∞

**Imagine a tomato plant feeling the need to produce the perfect tomato** and, rather than simply understanding that calling and allowing it to develop naturally, tries to control the sun and rain and to convince the farmer to fertilize the soil in a way the plant considers best. All of its energy and effort go into its own struggles to ensure the perfection of the object it is to produce, rather than allowing its existing systems – which were created specifically to accomplish that goal – to function as they should, without personal will and knowing with supreme confidence that the tomato is on its way.

This is very similar to your own situation. You are so anxious about your good unfolding exactly as you think it should that you have worked yourself into a state of confusion and fear and panic. Let go of the reins. They already are in my hands. My intention, like yours, is to allow and enable the perfection of the divine plan to unfold effortlessly in your life.

Let go of the need to make things happen according to the needs of your ego; relax and experience total peace; and let me work my wonders. Perfection is your essence. Rest in it; see it as your true identity; accept it; and allow your life to unfold through it.

You already are perfection, for you are my creation. You do not need to create your own perfection as you think it should be. Relax and let me carry the burden. That is how it was meant to be. You are loved. Go out into this day joyously and peacefully, for that is your nature. Expect perfection, for that is your entitlement. Abandon the fear and cast it on me, for I will gladly bear your burdens. Accept the blessings.

∞

**You do not need to know the next steps in the journey.** You do not need to struggle. You do not need to understand. Your role is simply to allow.

"But I must take action on the physical plane," you are saying, "or I will have no role at all." This, of course, is true, but you do not need to consciously figure out what the action is to be, and you certainly do not need to concern yourself with the ultimate outcome. You will be guided and directed, as you always have been.

Let go of the need to control or understand. What if you were to replace those with experiencing wonder in the moment – with simply having fun? That is hard for you even to imagine at this moment, but it truly is what you should be allowing to happen.

∞

**Think about train travel.** On a train, you do not need a road map. You do not need to concern yourself with which highways to take, or which turns to make, or where to spend the night, or when to re-fuel – as you do when you are driving your own car. Rather, you know that all of these matters have already been decided, and you let go of concern about them. You entrust the engineer and the other people who work on the train with the responsibility for getting you where you need to go and for making sure that your physical needs are met. You are able to enjoy the experience of the journey with the total assurance that you will arrive at your destination.

Make your life and the process of claiming and accepting the good that is yours a wonderful journey by rail. I will make the way for you, and it will become clear to you. Rest easy in the confidence that you will realize your goals. You may not have been able to find the way easily on you own, but you no longer have to fret over it.

Let go of the concern over each little step along the way and leave that to me. Know that you will arrive at your destination, and that I will make the way for you. Let go of the thought that you, as a human, need to do the deeds on your own, and accept the truth that my spirit, operating within you, will do them for you, if you only will let go of your need to direct the process. With God, all things are possible. Climb on board and enjoy the journey.

∞

**Simply understand and accept and celebrate the facility of it all.** Recognize and remember that all you need do, ultimately, is to allow your true spiritual beingness – who you really are – to take over and guide the way. All of your struggles and frustrations are a factor of your human mind's reluctance and resistance to letting go of its need to be in control and make things happen.

Your human identity is not evil or sinister or plotting against you. Its intentions are good, for it wants what it perceives to be in your best interests. But it is that part of your beingness whose vision and understanding are obscured by the illusions to which it has ascribed power or influence. It is not trying to bring you problems – it simply functions from such a limited perspective that its intentions seem unreachable.

Stop, always, to recognize and acknowledge this truth and then simply let go of the needs you are perceiving through your human mind to figure things out and make them happen. The things you desire to influence are not negative. You believe them to be in your best interests, but your perspective is so limited that the obvious is invisible.

Remember and accept and understand that your true beingness is always operating on the spiritual plane, where miracles abound and all things are possible. There are no limitations of any kind. You are there – the real you. Meditate on this truth and feel the light and love and joy and peace of the Kingdom. This is the real you. It has no limitations at all. Allow it to set your intentions, rather than your human mind. You will know the difference, because there will be no struggle, no interference.

∞

**Not becoming attached to your human mind's determination about how things should work out** is an interesting challenge. On the one hand, you know the value and importance of setting goals and visioning and holding those desires in your mind and heart. And on the other is the certainty that with God all things are possible – and that I work in mysterious ways, my wonders to perform.

There is a delicate balance between the will of the egoic consciousness and your ultimate good. Ultimately, as always, it is a question of trust.

Growth and understanding do not follow the linear path that is comforting to the human mind. As you are able to release the need to control the specifics, the outcomes become more spectacular – and perfect – than your egoic mind could ever have conceived.

Perfection is the ultimate truth. If you can, at the very core of your being, accept perfection, then surrender is the only course of action for your life. The human mind perceives limitations where there are none. But that perception causes struggle, and struggle causes pain. Pain and perfection are mutually exclusive.

∞

**Release your hands from those levers of control that do not even exist**, and smile at the irony of your having spent so much of this lifetime trying to manage them to bring about outcomes that your conscious mind has considered appropriate.

And is it not interesting that, while struggling so seriously to have things evolve in "your" way, you have carried emotional doubts that they ever would? Your human mind has been at once stressing and straining to have its own way (rather than knowing that perfection is constantly unfolding), and at the same time working to sabotage those efforts. Think of the absurdity and frustration of it all. The more you have struggled to have things evolve the way you have convinced yourself they should, the greater have become your doubts and fears.

Let go of all of this conflict and simply be. You understand that this is the "path of least resistance" (another interesting phrase), and that your resistance is limiting the expression of your good and your ability to live this phase of your life in the way that will bring the greatest peace and joy and love and benefit to you and to the physical world. It is limiting your expression of your true being (be-ing). Simply be. Use your conscious mind constructively, as a conduit for your true expression. No more struggle, no more strife. As you release your hold on the levers – and the levers themselves – you release all obstructions to the effortless flow.

Go and be at peace. Be joyous. Let my light shine through your eyes. They are a channel for light. There is no such thing as fear. It is a concoction of your ego. If it does not exist, it cannot harm you. You are blessed, and a blessing. Shine your light. And *enjoy* the journey.

∞

**You do not need to know.** How difficult it is for you to understand and accept that. You do not need to know. You are not a free agent, fending for yourself in the world, needing to prove yourself or take this action or that. You are part of eternal goodness, of perfection and peace.

Ask for my guidance and for the assistance of the legions, and then *know*, without any need to comprehend it, that all is well, that you are provided for, that all of your needs are met, that your conscious human mind is not responsible for figuring it all out.

Simply release and let go and surrender all of the confusion and uncertainty, for they are a concoction of your human mind's reaction to the illusions. Simply allow me to work through you, to express goodness and perfection through you.

This is a glorious, enjoyable adventure you are on. And it is glorious and enjoyable because perfection is all there is. Accept it. Simply accept it and enjoy the journey. Enjoy it!

Enjoyment is not possible in the midst of emotional turmoil or uncertainty. Peace and perfection and joy are certain. All you need do is surrender the fight, the struggle, and then accept them, live them, experience them without question or pause.

Smile and relax, for all is perfect. Everything is taken care of. All of your needs are being met in every moment.

∞

**For once and for all simply let go and trust and allow.** And I am speaking here, of course, of your human identity. It can relax and enjoy the spectacle and rejoice in the manifestation of all the desires we have expressed together.

Yes, it truly is that simple, that perfect, that effortless. Give thanks in the certainty that all is well, all is perfect, all is in divine order, and then simply let go and trust and allow – and enjoy and praise and celebrate and give thanks.

Enough of these dreary days of uncertainty! Simply get out of the way and let the good times roll! I love you. Be at peace and enjoy the journey.

∞

**Allow your entire being to experience peace and trust and surrender** – and the total absence of fear or need to control.

When you can completely accept the fact that you are not in control and simply know – without even a smidgen of doubt – that your good is already present, already part of you, you will experience the Kingdom.

Do not deny yourself the understanding of perfection any longer. Your conscious mind accepts and believes, but your subconscious resists. Bring it under control and allow your soul its freedom, and miracles will surround you forever.

∞

**The peace is in the flow.** Simply allow it. The flow is always present –
in you and in all incarnated souls.

As you peel away the struggles and attempts to understand and
control and make things happen, the peace and blessings of the flow are
easily accessible. All you need do is simply acknowledge and accept the
flow and allow yourself to surrender to it.

The flow, of course, is the Kingdom, but terminology can at
times be limiting, for it creates pictures or definitions in your human
mind that carry with them the mind's own interpretations, based on its
experiences and biases.

There is no need to define or interpret. Simply accept and
allow, accept and allow. All your needs are met. They will flow into
your life much more effortlessly as you define them clearly and
precisely.

∞

**Be at peace in the world and accept your good.** Rejoice in this new
day and the blessings it will bring. Expect miracles. Expect abundance.
Expect perfection, for that is all there is.

Claim your entitlement, and then carry on, comfortably and
peacefully and joyously and confidently, knowing that it is yours – and
you need not even know the specifics of what it is. Simply know that it
is perfect and for your highest good, and that all is well.

Life need not be a struggle. In fact, struggle should not exist at
all if you have surrendered your will and your need to be in control and
make things happen.

Simply accept the freedom and perfection of the Kingdom, for
you are experiencing it now when you simply let go and allow. How
easy and effortless and perfect it all is.

*You are in the Kingdom.* Now. Forever. You need not make the
transition from the physical realm to the spiritual in order to experience

it. You will, of course, make that transition, but the Kingdom is here for you now, as well.

Celebrate. Accept. Trust. Allow. Be. The path is unobstructed. The doors are open. You are experiencing the perfection of the Kingdom.

∞

**Accept the calm of this day.** Accept the perfection, the blessings that are always coming your way. Be at peace and be joyous, for those are your expressions of me.

Allow the goodness to flow. You are one with the blessings that are yours. Your life, and the entire universe, are in the perfection of divine order. Your human mind can be at peace, yet alive with receptivity to my guidance and love.

Claim and accept your good and look forward to it with eager anticipation, but do not become attached to a specificity. You are entitled to your good, no questions asked. But your human mind cannot discern the exact nature of that good that would serve you best during this journey in the physical world. Leave that up to me.

Go out into your day today with a smile on your face and love in your heart, and experience the peace that is yours always. I love you, my child.

∞

**Remain calm in the face of all adversity**, for all is well, all is perfection.

Simply accept and expect. Accept your true identity as a spiritual being – a perfect expression of me in the physical world. Accept perfection and divine order – completely, without any doubt or reservation – and know that everything, in your life and in the universe, is working together for good. Accept the goodness and abundance and blessings and miracles which are your entitlement as a child of God. Accept my guidance and direction, for it is always available, whether you ask or not (though the act of asking makes it easier for you to receive.)

And then eagerly expect or anticipate all that you have accepted. Know without any doubt or reservation that your true spiritual beingness is always in the Kingdom. Allow all things to be perfectly orchestrated and to unfold effortlessly in your life. Accept the goodness and blessings and abundance that you at times continue to resist, for they are yours for the asking and the expecting – and of course you need not know the how or when or what.

Simply expect and wait with the certainty of eager anticipation. And, of course, expect the loving guidance and direction that are always available to you – in every moment of your journey. If that guidance is perfect (which, of course, it is) and you accept it and trust it and follow it, the pathway will always be open and unobstructed and perfect for you.

Glorious things are happening on your behalf. Expect, accept, and allow. I love you.

∞

**Do not forget your unity with me and with all of my creation.** Do not forget to celebrate it and rejoice in it and to expect the good which you desire. Remember to be joyous and enthusiastic – even when circumstances show no cause for doing so.

All of this, once again, is a discussion of discipline and commitment. If you are committed to realizing and experiencing and expressing your unity with me, you will never forget it or take it for granted. Your life's desires are my will for you. Celebrate that fact and remember to accept your good.

The good which you desire is beginning to flow into your life more freely. Accept it, welcome it, rejoice in it, and expect it with joy and enthusiasm. Give thanks for the opportunities that are presented to you and recognize them as opportunities to express my goodness in the world. Be at peace and filled with joy as you do so. Accept your good with peace and praise and gratitude.

Your life is a blessing to the world. Realize and accept that truth and live your life with joy. You are very loved.

∞

**Allow peace to enfold you.** Feel your connection with the universe, with me. Allow your egoic being to release its grip on you.

Remind yourself of the effortlessness and perfection of the process of manifestation from the invisible to the visible. Nature has no resistance whatsoever, and magnificence unfolds with no stress or strain. Your human consciousness, for so much of your life, has distracted you from seeing and understanding the simplicity and profundity of that truth.

As you release the resistance to perfect unfoldment, it has no barriers. Do you not see the perfection? If it can manifest so magnificently in the tiny leaves of a fern, that offers no resistance whatsoever, with how much more grandeur can it be expressed through you?

∞

**Ask for blessings, for they are yours.** Ask to be blessed, knowing that it will happen, and then start by expecting goodness.

Let go of the tribulations of your mind. Its fears and doubts and worries and paranoia and insecurity. Stop! You are my child, in whom I am well pleased.

Be open to the flow. Neither force it nor resist it. Simply accept it. Ask for the blessings. Ask for the guidance. Then let go of the need to determine what or how or when. Let go of the struggle. It truly is an effortless surrender.

∞

**Believe without doubt** that the good which we have desired together, as well as blessings which I desire for you that you have not yet even become aware of, will be made manifest in your life at the perfect moment. This belief must be just as strong and unwavering when there is no evidence at all available to your human consciousness that blessings will be made manifest as when the blessings have appeared.

Know that, because you are one with the flow of divine life, which is a perfect, never-ending stream of blessings that come from me as the source of all good, you are *always* at one with the blessings themselves. This, of course, is on a spiritual level. On the physical plane where you are residing, this reality can become obscured very easily, which can serve as a stimulus for you to allow all types of negative thoughts (doubt, fear, discouragement, lack, inadequacy, etc.) to take over your human consciousness.

You can bring your own good into the physical world. You can give birth to it through your consciousness. It is easy and natural and logical and perfect. If you believe – *truly* believe, with no doubts whatsoever – that this is so, you will begin to see wonderful things happen in your life. They may seem amazing to you at the outset, but you soon will understand them as the logical outpicturing of your true beliefs.

∞

**Rejoice.** Truly rejoice and give thanks and accept and allow your good to unfold before your very eyes. You do not need to know the how or when or where – just as you did not know exactly when or where you would see the first flower burst through the ground and add its beauty to the landscape, or on which tree you would see the first leaf barely beginning to open up. You knew that their manifestation was assured, as is the manifestation of the good you have awaited for such a seemingly long time.

Can you totally accept that truth, without any doubt or fear or reservation? Can you allow that total acceptance to give you the freedom and confidence to finally let go of any remaining doubt or fear or frustration or need to force the issue? Simply accept and allow. Live in certainty and peace and joy. The surrender you now will experience is not one of giving up hope. It is surrendering your uncertainty, of discontinuing the battle.

Just as you are watching the glory of nature unfold before your eyes in total splendor, peacefulness and perfection – without any struggle or any need for anyone's human mind to try to control – so are you now beginning to witness and experience and rejoice in the perfect, effortless unfoldment and manifestation of the goodness you have been desiring (and I have been desiring for you, through you) – the opportunities to use your gifts to help bring joy and peace and love and understanding to the world, to experience the abundance that your intellect has always known was there, but that you had not allowed to unfold before you.

Rejoice, for spring has sprung in your life. The newness and perfection are real. Bless you. Accept and allow and enjoy the blessings as they flow forth.

∞

**Take it for granted.** Know that your good will be made manifest in your life. The origin of the concept of taking something for granted is interesting. In the days when certain persons had the authority to approve requests or wishes submitted by others, they would "grant" the wish – or give their approval to its realization. To take something for granted, then, means to know that the request has been approved and that the good that was asked for will become a reality. Today, the term has been changed somewhat to have an "of course" meaning, where one does not even think about the possibility of something not happening.

Either definition will work perfectly for you. You must remove all doubt about the perfect outworking of your dreams and move forward in total confidence, knowing with full certainty that I am in charge and that, with me, all things are possible – to him who believeth. If all of your doubts are gone, and you are taking the manifestation of the good you have desired "for granted," then your belief is rock solid.

Think about how different your day-to-day existence would be if you knew with full certainty that you will achieve your goals – that the requests and wishes you have asked for *will* be "granted." Worry about these things will have no purpose. Timing will be irrelevant. You will need only to proceed ahead each day with full confidence, taking those steps which are necessary in order to continue your progress – and, of course, to enjoy each moment to the fullest.

Can you bring yourself to this absolute belief and conviction? Can you let go of the worry and agony and concern and frustration that seem to be habitual preoccupations for you? If someone were to call and tell you that you had won one of the sweepstakes you enter, would you think for a moment about whether to accept your winnings? I am telling you that your wishes and requests will be granted. Express praise and thanksgiving, accept the granting of your wish with graciousness, and move forward in your life, eagerly anticipating the manifestation of your good. What could be more simple?

∞

**This is a time of great change – change you can only begin to see or imagine.** Allow it. Simply allow it and welcome it and give thanks for it, knowing that it is unfolding in divine perfection.

You don't need to know the specifics. When you go to a movie, you might have a general idea about the story – or you might have none at all. But you settle into the darkness along with others who will experience it with you, and you allow that story to unfold. There will be surprises and laughter and uncertainty, and sometimes even terror, but you are in a comfortable setting, knowing that all is well, and allowing the storyline to unfold.

Do the same with your life on earth. You are safe and protected. All is well. Just as you do in a movie theatre, you feel no need to control the outcome or how the plot unfolds. You know that it has been developed by writers and directors and producers and special effects people whose areas of expertise are far greater than yours, and you do not attempt to intervene because you know all is well – and because you know and understand that your ability as a human observing the unfoldment need only sit back and allow.

Your life journey is orchestrated and directed and produced in perfection – in ways your human consciousness could never even begin to imagine. And all you need do is observe and enjoy and allow. Yes, you will be directed and guided to the proper arena in which to observe the spectacle, and to the specific seat from which you will watch it, and you will need to make a commitment to be there – and to contribute financially for the opportunity to participate in the spectacle. But you as a human need not (nor should you even try) struggle or squirm or try to figure it all out.

Simply participate and show up and enjoy. There are no worries, no uncertainties, no doubts or concerns. You need only show up and be there, trusting that all will unfold perfectly and effortlessly and as it should.

∞

**The best is yet to come.** It is important that you remember this and anticipate it. It will always be true – the good which awaits you is even better than you can imagine. No matter how good your blessings seem to you, greater ones always await you. If you can accept this, your sense of anticipation will always be keen and enthusiastic. You never can truly "arrive" in this physical life, for you always are growing in your understanding of truth, and as your understanding increases, so will your access and receptivity to the infinite blessings of the universe to which you are entitled.

This is why your soul should always be open to new yearnings and new understanding. As you grow in understanding, not only will your desires continue to expand and to be realized, but you will become ever increasingly aware of your unity with me.

Your life should never be static. There is always much to learn and do and try. Never stop reaching, for there will always be even greater blessings to reach for. Your life is in divine order, and all is well. Bless you.

# Other Books by Jack Armstrong:

*Lessons from the Source:*
*A Spiritual Guidebook for Navigating Life's Journey*

*More Lessons from the Source:*
*Practical Wisdom for Enjoying Life's Journey*

*From the Source: An Introduction to Channeling*

Life's journey is one we all share and navigate together. We are never alone. To get more information, find other products and services by Jack Armstrong, and join a growing online community of loving adventurers sharing experiences and finding the joy in their journey, please visit:

**www.lessonsfromthesource.com**

www.ingramcontent.com/pod-product-compliance
Lightning Source LLC
Chambersburg PA
CBHW071803020426
42331CB00008B/2386